Sadaf Sagheer
Kashir Asghar

Suit Up

The concept of self through the communal embeddedness of a James Bond brandscape

LAP LAMBERT Academic Publishing

Impressum / Imprint
Bibliografische Information der Deutschen Nationalbibliothek: Die Deutsche Nationalbibliothek verzeichnet diese Publikation in der Deutschen Nationalbibliografie; detaillierte bibliografische Daten sind im Internet über http://dnb.d-nb.de abrufbar.
Alle in diesem Buch genannten Marken und Produktnamen unterliegen warenzeichen-, marken- oder patentrechtlichem Schutz bzw. sind Warenzeichen oder eingetragene Warenzeichen der jeweiligen Inhaber. Die Wiedergabe von Marken, Produktnamen, Gebrauchsnamen, Handelsnamen, Warenbezeichnungen u.s.w. in diesem Werk berechtigt auch ohne besondere Kennzeichnung nicht zu der Annahme, dass solche Namen im Sinne der Warenzeichen- und Markenschutzgesetzgebung als frei zu betrachten wären und daher von jedermann benutzt werden dürften.

Bibliographic information published by the Deutsche Nationalbibliothek: The Deutsche Nationalbibliothek lists this publication in the Deutsche Nationalbibliografie; detailed bibliographic data are available in the Internet at http://dnb.d-nb.de.
Any brand names and product names mentioned in this book are subject to trademark, brand or patent protection and are trademarks or registered trademarks of their respective holders. The use of brand names, product names, common names, trade names, product descriptions etc. even without a particular marking in this works is in no way to be construed to mean that such names may be regarded as unrestricted in respect of trademark and brand protection legislation and could thus be used by anyone.

Coverbild / Cover image: www.ingimage.com

Verlag / Publisher:
LAP LAMBERT Academic Publishing
ist ein Imprint der / is a trademark of
OmniScriptum GmbH & Co. KG
Heinrich-Böcking-Str. 6-8, 66121 Saarbrücken, Deutschland / Germany
Email: info@lap-publishing.com

Herstellung: siehe letzte Seite /
Printed at: see last page
ISBN: 978-3-659-61137-7

Copyright © 2014 OmniScriptum GmbH & Co. KG
Alle Rechte vorbehalten. / All rights reserved. Saarbrücken 2014

Dedication

To my parents, Iffat and Sagheer Janjua thank you for your endless support and unwavering confidence in me. Who I am and whatever I have achieved is all because of you two.

Acknowledgements

A huge thank you to my supervisor Kashir Asghar, firstly Thank you for increasing your work load and agreeing to supervise me, trusting I knew what I was doing even when I was questioning it and making sure I stuck to deadlines. I'd also like to thank both sets of my grandparents for all their prayers and constant reminders of how special I am. Shout outs to all my people, my brothers Hamza and Jawad thank you guys for helping out, taking dictations and typing for me when I got bored of it. My support system Maham, Adan, Sheraz, Zain thank you for not letting me procrastinate too much and providing me just the right amount of distractions to keep me sane. I happen to have the best cheering crowd ever. Also thank you Akhtar Rehman for your guidance and support.

Preface

In the recent years the trend of brand placements and brand patronage in films has become quite the norm, much importance has been given to the brands endorsed through films and television. The literature talking about films as brands has emerged and significant importance has been given to the endorsed brand's role in creating a brandscape where the fans not only relate to the movies but also to other fans. This research takes the idea of a film brandscape and uses the James Bond franchise to study its ability in creating a brandscape by focusing on the fashion brands patronized in the franchise the research explores how the fans use those fashion brands to create or morph meanings for themselves in their daily lives.

Table of Contents

Chapter: 1 Bond, James Bond

1. Bond, James Bond

A brandscape is an ideological landscape where the tribe members have shared beliefs, values, associations and aspirations due to the brands they consume (Salzer & Strannegård, 2010). Postmodern consumers looking for both communal and individualistic experiences (Simmons, 2008) feel a sense of belonging based on their associations with the brandscape based on the brands they consume. The brandscape is composed of visual expressions and the consumption of brands becomes an act of expression of self (Salzer & Strannegård, 2010). Brands basically are a story of the corporation the brand represents, conveying a message of the corporation *(ibid)*.

Films at the fundamental level can be regarded as brands, as films are commercial products with symbolic meanings (O'Reilly & Kerrigan, 2013). Films provide the audiences with simulated moments; the film brand narratives involve the audiences and make them feel the emotions of the characters (Woodside, et al., 2013). It provides a platform for the audiences to relive the experiences through the archetypes presented in the movies one of the common archetypes presented in the movies is the hero archetype *(ibid)* the hero or protagonist in movies is a construction of a particular identity, embodies particular cultural values (O'Reilly & Kerrigan, 2013) and represents a classic figure that is prominent in people's minds (Woodside, et al., 2013).

Cooper, Schembri and Miller (cited in Woodside, et al., 2013) explain the protagonist or hero archetype by using the example of the James Bond charcter, a typical protagonist not only inspires people to like him but also he aspires people to want to be like him. The character aspirations that people have with James Bond's character brand are not just reflected in the picture that James Bond presents but also the products or brands that James Bond uses, over the years James Bond has been associated with many brands be it fashion brands such Tom Ford or Turnbull and Asser, Omega watches or other brands such as Aston Matin cars, Hienken beer and Sony (O'Reilly & Kerrigan, 2013).

Brand patronage and placements is a phenomena that is widely used by marketeers and talked about by researchers. Research on Film brandscapes and the placed brands in movies is mostly contextual and explanatory in nature, thus the impact of the placed and patronized brands in movies is not fully explored. This research builds on the theoretical foundations of the previous researches and uses the James Bond brandscape to explore the brandscape and how the fans use the brands associated with the Bond franchise to morph meanings to themselves and whether the associated brands have an impact on the purchase pattern of the Bond fans or not.

1.1 Overview of the chapters

Chapter two starts by talking about the ability of movies to impact audience both consciously and unconsciously, it explains the various archetypes present in the movies. It goes on to discuss how the films today are brands in their own right and the ability they have to develop associations in the form of tribes by providing the fans with a brandscape they consciously or unconsciously become a part of and relate to the other members in the same brandscape. The chapter then uses the example of James Bond franchise as a brandscape and talks about the protagonist James Bond and how the brands he uses and styles he adopts aspire people to follow suit. The chapter is concluded by presenting the research question and the research aims and objectives based on the gap in the literature.

Chapter three talks about the methodology used for this research, highlighting the various steps of this research and it also includes a detailed account and explanations of the methods chosen and used in this study.

Chapter four highlights the findings of this research based on the different methods used for this research. It covers various aspects of the study based on the different methods adopted and the results from the chosen methods.

Chapter five sums up and discusses the findings from the previous chapters. It takes into account the findings from different methods used and compares the results in terms of similarities and differences between findings.

Chapter: 2 How it all began...

2. How it all began

Over most of this century movies composed of ordinary themes, presented in ordinary ways through brilliant acting have influenced more people than anything else, through the ability to shift perspectives and stimulating conceptual flexibility (Pandey, 2012). Schutz (cited in Wiley, 2003) talks about the concept of multiple worlds or multiple realities, the main everyday world and the secondary world of arts and movies, where we enter with an act of faith or willing suspended disbelief, invoked by the presented images, developed through archetypical characters within truncated scenarios (Sementelli, 2009). Ayikoru and Park (cited in Pandey, 2012) talk about the emotionality and stimulation of the senses through imagery and visualization and its potential to move from imagination to reality and possibly vice versa. The louder, larger than life nature of movies induces the audience in a secondary world, where time is sped up and the audience go through an emotional journey which surpasses the real life emotions of their typical day (Wiley, 2003).

Woodside & Megehee (cited in Ko & Lee, 2013) talk about the unconsious impact of innate stories that all humans carry, which are represented by archetypical forces. Studying Jung's archetypes in movies, Vogler (Woodside, et al., 2013) states that all stories are constituted of a few common structural themes and elements, found universally in fairytales, myths, dreams and movies. The most common archetype in stories for cinema is the protagonist/ hero archetype, a classic figure who plays a prominent role in people's minds with his/her inspiring ideals and protection of the weak which makes him bigger than self (Woodside, et al., 2013). Dowd (cited in Dowd, 2003) analyzes the ideological properties of *Jerry McGuire* that presents social consensus and reinforces the existence of social conditions by the manipulation of ideological themes and utopian dreams.

The Hollywood archetypes underwent a subtle change, which was evident in the so called 'new Hollywood' compared to the old, pre war Hollywood (Hudson & Tung, 2010) where movies changed their potrayal of executives as villains. Prior to World War II the depiction of American corporate executive was simple. Drucker (cited in Spector, 2008) talks about the executive as little more than euphemism for 'the boss', Charlie Chaplin's movie, *Modern Times (1936)* potrayed just that image, a steel company president playing with a jigsaw puzzle and reading Sunday funnies at his office, his executive responsibilities were presented as a parody of scientific management where he interupts worker's breaks and orders speed ups of the assembly line. Producer/ director Frank Capara who had thrived with story lines of small town protagonists pitted against fat cat corporate villains had to drop the story lines potraying corporate executives as villains. Movies like Billy Wilder's *Sabrina* showing corporate executives as protagonists, who considered industries to be the new revoloution and money just a by product of work took over Hollywood. However after the war Capara came back with *It's a wonderful life* pittying a greedy banker against a small town loans and saving institute (Spector, 2008).

Consumers expectations are not consious, the stories they experience are repeated in the collective unconsious and they bring meaning and connect them to the community that they belong to (Woodside, et al., 2013). The repeated patterns and images in the stories make the audience creatures of action rather than reflection, urging them to forego serious thoughts. Films like any other product have to attract the consumer's attention inorder to sentient the audience to their art's affirmative qualities (Dowd, 2003). The existing literature on box office highlights the important characteristics that help the studios in gaining attention of the audience which are: movie characteristics, post filming studio action and external factors, movie characteristics include the personnel of the movie, the cast and the crew, its star power (Thurau, et al., 2006). The filming studio activities may include all the marketing activities that the studio indulges in to reach its target audience (ibid).

Films, at a basic level may as well be regarded as brands (O'Reilly & Kerrigan, 2013), Murphy (cited in Moor, 2007) defines brands as a unique property, developed over time, with both tangible and intangible attributes which appropriately differentiate products that would otherwise have been similar, and provides consumers with a simplified route map when faced with bewildering choices. Films are startegic assets for their firms, are offered for sale as commercial products that carry intellectual property rights to differentiate them from other films (O'Reilly & Kerrigan, 2013). Guyon (cited in Delassus & Descotes, 2012) points that brand equity comprises of two components, the functional components and the symbolic components. Functional dimensions describe how the product or service meets the consumer needs, while the symbolic dimensions are intangible aspects such as image associations (Delassus & Descotes, 2012). Jasson (cited in Salzer & Strannegård, 2010) states that whereas the functional values are regarded as a product's material or physical qualities, the expressive side of a brand refers to its immaterial values and images. Even though it could be argued that the functional values are expressive in some sense, and vice versa, a distinction between the two can be made Hence, in a marketplace that to an increasing extent is concerned with the production and consumption of signs, the brand is not only a marker of identification, but also something that is consumed in its own right. As Baudrillard (cited in Salzer & Strannegård, 2010) puts it, consumption, today has become nothing more than a 'signifying play'. By infusing products with emotional, ideological and aesthetic values, the idea is to create brands that differentiate the products beyond their immediate apparent functional value. In line with most consumer behaviour theories, branding is regarded as a strategy for creating positive attitudes that ultimately generate the desired outcome: a consumer purchase (Salzer & Strannegård, 2010). Kerrigan (cited in O'Reilly & Kerrigan, 2013) talks about two key characteristics that determine the film's engagement with the market place: marketability and playability. The first denotes how attractive a film is to its target audience, whereas the later signifies how well the audience responds to the film once they commit to watching it. Marketability is associated with the clarity of the message and correlation of various brand elements that are presented in the marketing campaign through functional aspects such as posters, consumers draw meanings from a film's brand elements based on the previous exposure to the same brand elements such as actors, directors. However playability deals with the future sense making, how the preconceived meanings associated with the brand elements change based on the actual consumption of the film and how the post film consumption meanings associated with the brand elements differ from the preconceived meanings *(ibid)*.

The film brand is artistic as well as commercial, and these values can not be decoupled easily. Artistic elements of the film brand includes the people brands, that play a role in the development of a film such as the actors, directors or screenwriters, as well as the storyline, the characters and even music. Some movies contain such strong characters that they become a brand in their own right, or the film's music might become so sucessful that it becomes a cue for the movie, which in itself can be a brand. On the commercial side the film might have sequels and prequels that can be regarded as brand extensions (O'Reilly & Kerrigan, 2013). These commercial elements of sequels and prequels play a vital role in reducing the risk that the consumer associates with trying out a new movie (Thurau, et al., 2006). As an indvidual considering to watch the film takes cues from both artistic and commercial aspects of the film, and analyzes the people aspect of the film (O'Reilly &

Kerrigan, 2013). For instance a person may look at a *Kevin Costner* poster and analyze whether the movie is a western or a part of *Star Trek* franchise (Thurau, et al., 2006). Levin et.al (cited in Thurau, et al., 2006) explains the personnel attractiveness of movie characteristics with the help of information economics and states that just as a brand name indicates a certain consistency or level of quality, the participation of particular people in the film, or the film belonging to a certain franchise may give out a sign of quality to the perspective audience. According to Jarvis et.al (cited in Thurau, et al., 2006) the personnel and cultural familarity of a film may help the film in a formative manner, however they are not correlated.

Branding plays a vital role in consiously constructing a concept of unique identity in the midst of competetive contexts and facilitates brand identification and its connection to specific consumers (Woodside, et al., 2013). With the shrinking of functional differences between brands, to the postmodern consumer the symbolic meaning associated with brands becomes more important than material utility, the postmodern consumer regards posessions as not just material beings but a means to construct a personal identity, possesions and material objects that a person owns or endorses acts as clues for indentification and differentiation to be used by the consumers and the consumers social group (Perez, et al., 2010) and hence the consumer patronizes brands that they believe compliment their personal identities *(ibid)* and regard brands as an extension to self identity and an indication of self worth (Lazarevic, 2012) as the consumer today uses his/her consumption and brand preferences to 'make up' or define who they are and who they want to be as the changing postmodern culture has lead the consumers away from the point where indentity was a static concept, today the identity is not considered as a thing but it is regarded as a project that is to be worked at, organized and managed (Shankar, et al., 2009). Brands play a vital role in this identity construction for the consumers (Perez, et al., 2010) brands talk to consumer's unconsious selves, and produce a powerful emotional response (Woodside, et al., 2013).

Cova and Pace (cited in Simmons, 2008) discuss the highly fragmented post modern, complex consumer, who does not need extreme reassurance or acceptance, but the postmodern consumer learns to live with and not be anxious about the realitivity and the half truths presented by the world, the postmodern consumer has the knowledge and has learned to co exist and live with his/her own finites beyond the pretensious and the nostalgia of absolute truths (Ligorio, 2004). The postmodern consumer seeks not just indvidualistic but also communal brand experiences, he/she does not potray a united central self but a jigsaw of multiple selves and preferences, consumption allows the post modern consumers to create more desireable self images (Simmons, 2008). Flrat and Shultz (cited in Simmons, 2008) talk about communal brand experiences and how the indvidualistic postmodern society of multiple shallow images has lead to a nostalgia for a momentarily belonging (Dionι´sio, et al., 2008).

This need to belong leads to tribes, Cova (cited in Dionι´sio, et al., 2008) introduces the word 'tribe' that refers to the recurrence of quasi archaic values and communal beliefs. Tribe, unlike a market segment is a network of heterogeneous people, in terms of gender, sex and income, who are alike not because of the same demographics but are linked due to their similar way of life. According to Cova (cited in Mitchell & Imrie, 2011) Consumer tribes are relatively a new concept in society and yet have made a an important impact on marketing theory. Consumer tribes unlike historical tribes have a new social order, wherein status within a tribe is achieved by different and specific values. They are grouped about something emotional rather than rational . Consumer tribes differ from the subcultures in the sense that their connections are much narrower, with similar beliefs, values or customs unlike the dominant societal culture, the term 'brand community' is an inadequate means of describing a tribe. A brand community is recognized as supporting a particular brand or product which contrasts with consumer tribes, which in some instances may diminish brand equity, similar to a consumer activist placing themselves in opposition to mainstream consumers (Mitchell & Imrie, 2011). Kozinets (cited in Mitchell & Imrie, 2011) states that there are two antecedents of tribal membership. First tribal membership provides a self identity and second it leads to communal associations and builds social relationships. This social embededness provides indvidual identity and self image. Tajfel (cited in Dionı´sio, et al., 2008) points out that without social affiliations, indviduals would not be able to form self images. According to Fisher & Wakefield (cited in Dionı´sio, et al., 2008) the stronger these social affiliations are the indvidual would be more likely to attribute the group's charcteristics to self and relate more to the other group members. Mun~ iz & Hamer (cited in Felix, 2012) talk about tribal members and how they define themselves by the brands that they consume as well as the brands they do not consume, and classify the availible brands as 'our' brands vs 'other' brands.

Branding in a non traditional context in the fictional world, an imaginary world that mimics the real world, can be witnessed in the imaginary world of theatre and movies where the consumers are a mere audience instead of actively involved participants (Muzellec, et al., 2012). However the changing market place and the shift in power from the producers to the consumer changes that, Cova (cited in Simmons, 2008) emphasizes that the postmodern consumer wants experiences that are based on collectivity and creativity. Thus the brands, even film brands have to allow the audiences a phenomenon of morphing symbolic associations and meaning alteration (Cova, et al., 2007) thus films are more than just a means of two dimensional representation of fantasy based on central themes *(ibid)*.

Baudrillard (cited in Simmons, 2008) talks about hyper real, simulated environments, where reality has collapsed and replaced by image illusions this fictionalization of reality leads the atomized postmodern indviduals to become the imitators of style that is prefabricated by the marketing system through the instrumental development of brand identity. The brand identifiers that consumers develop and discourse inorder to distinguish products in the marketplace which illustrates the importance of a brandscape, which is defined as a cultural landscape where brand meanings are developed (Salzer & Strannegård, 2010) this ability to distinguish is particularly important for film brandscapes where the film brands compete or compliment brand meanings in the minds of consumers (O'Reilly & Kerrigan, 2013). The emerging concept of postmodern brandscape implies a shift in focus from function to expression (Salzer & Strannegård, 2010) where actual reality is substituted by media reality, fact is substituted by fiction and fantasy. The film brandscape stimulates brand construction through the archetypes that the consumers use to relive their experiences and create meaning for themselves through the films they watch (Woodside, et al., 2013). Deighton et al. (cited in Woodside, et al., 2013) states that from the viewpoint of brands, brand narratives and images can involve the audience and make them feel the emotions and concerns of the characters involved, using the concept of suspension of disbelief where the audience accepts the premises of the images and storyline overlooking the inconsistencies and plot holes (Sementelli, 2009) and a specific behavior is evoked in the audience without them being consious of it (Woodside, et al., 2013) as flims not just infleuence the audience but seek to change values and beliefs (Spector, 2008).

Cooper, Schembri, and Miller (cited in Woodside, et al., 2013) explore the hero archetype by giving an example of the James Bond movie stating that the ideological structure of the movie presents the archetypical ideology of a heroic character and his journey. Vogler (cited in Woodside, et al., 2013) states that the hero archetype has traits that not only inspire people but makes them want to be like him. The typical protagonist experiences an accident or comes across something that leads to the protagonis's quest or journey that he takes which results in an awakening for the protagonist (Ko & Lee, 2013). Fifty years after Sean Connery uttered the words "Bond, James Bond" (Nittins, 2011) the James Bond as we knew him has undergone many changes, from the global yet reassuring Anglo Saxon hero, who carried his cold war scars, was always in control, and never broke a sweat no matter what the circumstances, the larger than life protagonist's control never wavered, the fleeting glimpses of vulnerability he showed were intimate and yet it did not pierece the aura of control the larger than life character was surrounded by, Bond's 'license to kill' allowed him to shy away from the wreckage of his finished jobs (Weiner, et al., 2011) from Sean Connery to Daniel Craig, Bond has evolved fitting himself into an era where heroes are armed with everything but certainity, Bond has outgrown his origins of a 'gentleman spy' and the revisionism has lead to an ambivalent, tortured, loner protagonist who wears his blood, angst, vengence and despair silently but visibly, a by product no doubt of the post 9/11 culture that no doubt he has been called to serve *(ibid)*.

In the film history, the James Bond franchise is one of the most successful projects, Bond character is one of the most famous popular culture icons, that is embedded in everyone's memory even the people who have not been in direct contact with the paper or print Bond (Nittins, 2011). According to Kerrigan (cited in O'Reilly & Kerrigan, 2013) franchise can be identified as a recycled, repositioned and repackaged film product, which originates as a line extension product for instance the James Bond film series is a very succesful franchise originates from a British novel by Ian Fleming. Where James Bond is a British secret service agent who is licensed to kill on the agency's behalf. This British secret service agent also plays to the country of origin theory in quintessentially representing a spy who guards British interests. The British country of origin provides a centeral theme to the Bond franchise and that's how Bond is presented to the audience. Though quintensentially British, James Bond travels to various exotic locations for his quests such as Jamaica (Dr No), Japan (you only live twice), Thailand (the man with the golden gun) and Czech Republic (Casino Royale) (O'Reilly & Kerrigan, 2013).

Klub kinoputeshestvennikov' is the Russian term that is used to describe how film locations influence the tourists and the exotic locations the movies are shot at become

favored tourist spots, As a rule, every film in the James
the James Bond series shows a certain country. As soon
as someone says Phuket, beautiful island Phi Phi and
then, you remember the movie about James Bond, and
the people understand and want to go there (Lysikova,
2012).

Despite all the exotic locations James Bond travels to, he
is presented as an authentic British icon, even if Bond
franchise is a product of American 'Hollywood' cinema,
many of the product placements in the film series are
British, majority of the films are filmed in Britain, with
British crews and sound stages (Nittins, 2011). The
Britain country of origin or COO effect, which is the
overall perception the consumers form of products from
certain countries based on the consumer's prior
perception of the country, acts as an information cue and
activates the antecedent knowledge of the consumers
which acts as a factor in the evaluation of the brand
(Chryssochoidis, et al., 2007). The COO image effect
acts as an extrinisic cue or image variable that arouses a
purely emotional response in the consumers (Bloemer, et
al., 2009).

Cooper et.al (cited in O'Reilly & Kerrigan, 2013) has
identified three dominant characteristics or three brand
narratives evident in James Bond the hero, the outlaw

and the lover. The Bond character brand is juxtaposed to the character villains that are intent on world domination and James Bond the hero puts a stop to it. James Bond is a representation of power, a financial power that not only buys fast cars, expensive watches and what not but that power is also witnessed in the confidence James Bond exudes. His attire or expensive suits, in a typical Hollywood fashion signify power. The dress or rather the suit of success is unambiguously same in all such Hollywod films where the powerful men are represented by the expensive suits they wear and the brands they associate themselves with (Panayiotou, 2012). Nobody can think of Bond without thinking of a tux, for more than four decades, six men have adorned the tuxedo with the ease of ordinary men wearing a T-shirt, each man adding his own edition to the classic, time has passed: cuff links, studs and cummerbunds have been added and removed but the tailored looks associated with Bond still stand out (Soller, 2011) the look signifies power for James Bond, from Terrence Young's self styled Bond in *Doctor No* (Weiner, et al., 2011) to Daniel Craig's Bond resplendent in his hand-tailored, perfect fit Tom Ford suit (Nittins, 2011).

When Sean Connery played Bond from 1962 to 1971, Connery proved over and over that a suit should and could be worn everyday of a man's life, a dark three piece suit with a slightly textured tie and a crisp white shirt and a matching pocket square were Connery's Bond signature look (Soller, 2011). As the 70's turned to the 80's Bond became trendier, wide collars and unbuttoned shirts and askew bow ties were Roger Moore's Bond signature look, as the years went by Bond's appearance added a casual tinge to his tailored clothing, Timothy Dalton's Bond depicted this casual and yet tailored look with wide lapels, lose tie and slightly over grown hair *(ibid)*. Pierce Brosnan's Bond brought relevance to the outerwear department, with his dark, plush overcoats Brosnan's Bond commanded respect. Ofcourse 007 wears suits often and so does Daniel Craig's Bond, a perfectly fit suit with clean lines, but a suit everyday, Craig's Bond questioned that, wearing casual jackets, jeans and sportswear *(ibid)*.

DeLorme & Reid (cited in Muzellec, et al., 2012) observes that the value of realism in movies through brand placements, where the placed products mirror the transformational starategy instead of the informational strategy is typically used in advertisments and infomercials, the product placement does not provide the viewers information regarding the product benefits and information about the brand but uses an entertainment context to engage the viewers (Lee, et al., 2010). The product placement is appreciated by the audiences, as it brings reality to a fictional or abstract environment (Muzellec, et al., 2012). The product placements, not only enhance the realism of the abstract movie environment, but many audience have indicated that the placed brands reinforce the integrity of the films and plays an important role in encouraging consumer engagement and absorption in the storyline while encouraging them to admire the naturalistic potrayals of the brands placed (Lee, et al., 2010). Bond is a secret agent, a master detective and yet more than that, Bond's style can not be denied or overlooked, from the 60's globe trotting, jet-setting secret agent to becoming the face of Omega watches, Bond's tastes and styles add a certain lush luxurious sophistication to the secret agent which have become characteristics often associated with James Bond (Weiner, et al., 2011).

Since 1962 a number of commercial brands have been associated with the Bond franchise such as Aston Martin an iconic British brand. Other brand associations include Omega watches, Heinken beer, Ford, Virgin Atlantic and Sony (O'Reilly & Kerrigan, 2013). These brand placements such as Aston Martin in Bond films provide a chance for the consumers to relate to their abstract heroes, when using the same brands as the celebrities they idolize, it also provides them with a sense of belonging to a virtual environment (Salzer &

Strannegård, 2010). When James bond receives his orders from M on his Sony Ericson phone, sips a glass of perfectly chilled Bollinger champagne and checks the time on his Omega watch while waiting for his Aston Martin to be brought around, consumers of the same brands feel a connection with the hero (Nittins, 2011).

The favourability of viewer response to the placements in films is associated with the positive valence and the prominence of how the product is presented and how it fits with the positive emotion evoked by the surrounding content (Lord & Gupta, 2010). Critics of using product palcements as a marketing means believe that the movie or the story line itself may cause distraction and the consumer may not be able to recall the presented products, However according to Morton & Friedman (cited in Lord & Gupta, 2010) the product characterisitcs and the charcters seen using the products affects the purchase decision which may increase the brand recall and generate a favourable response to the placed brands.

Research on developing films as brands is limited, and very little research has been conducted on the film brandscape as an ideological shared community of movie goers, the previous research on film brandscape is conceptual and theoretical in nature and provides a

31

means to associate meaning of a brandscape to film franchises. However there is no emperical research on the subject which creates a gap to be researched. Thus Salzer & Strannegård (2010) depiction of the brandscape as a cultural space where brand meanings are developed and circulated can be analyzed with respect to film brands to understand how the consumers morph the centeral themes of films as an extension to self and communal associations with other members. Though the past researchers have extensively used James Bond franchise and studied various aspects based on the films, and used the films as a reference point for many studies, in recent studies researchers such as Nittins (2011) have analyzed the James Bond franchise with respect to consumerism and product placements however most studies are contextual in nature and the ability of the patronized brands from the movies, to impact people's purchase patterns has not been studied.

Which leaves a gap in the literature to be researched, and paves a way to emperically test the literature and study the James Bond franchise inorder to understand how one of the most iconic movie franchise helps the consumer to morph self sybolism and meanings in their everyday life of both the global fandom members and Pakistani consumers. The success of the multiple brand placements and brand activations through the James Bond movies can be analyzed by seeking to understand whether all the brand placements are memorable to the consumers and whether or not those brand placements have made an impact by translating into consumer purchase patterns in terms of men's wear and accessories of the Pakistani consumers.

This book aims to emperically study the role of film brandscapes in providing symbolic, morphed identities to the consumers and seeks to understand the tribal behaviour of the members of the Bond tribe, whether or not the fandom is strong enough to build social and self symbolism and to study the purchase patterns and the brand usage of the Bond tribe members wether their charcter aspirations and influences are represented in their daily lives specifically brand patronage and product purchase patterns with respect to their fashion statements which would help to gauge how succesful Bond franchise as a tribe is and how successful the product and brand placements are with all the fandom members and whether the placed brands influence the Pakistani consumers in their consumption patterns and fashion decisions.

Research question

How does the communal embededness of a James Bond brandscape translate into the concept of self for its fandom members

Research objectives

- To analyze the morphed symbolism of the James Bond films in the everyday lives of its global fandom members
- To throughly explore the James Bond franchise in terms of the fashion trends adopted and the fashion brands patronized
- To evaluate the recall of fashion trends and brands used in the movies, and whether the fashion brands patronized affect the fashion aspirations of Pakistani fans

Chapter: 3 Methods adopted

3. Methods adopted

3.1 Introduction

This chapter explains the research design used for this book. Crotty (cited in Rageh, et al., 2013) highlights the four aspects that need to be considered when designing a research, firstly the epistemology of the study, in terms of the theory of knowledge embedded in the research, whether it is subjective or objective in nature, secondly what theoretical perspectives are there behind the methodological preference in question, whether it is based on positivism, postpositivism, interpretivism or critical theory. The third aspect is the methodological design or the strategic plan of action that would be used in the research in terms of whether the research would be experiential, survey based or ethnographic in nature, finally the methods or techniques of processes would be used such as interviews, focus groups etc *(ibid)*.

3.2 Nature of the research

The objective of this research was to evaluate different aspects of the James Bond brandscape from the brand placements and brand patronge in the movies and how the brand placements are used by the Bond fandom members to morph meanings in their everyday lives. The research also used fashion brands in the various Bond movies and emperically studied the recall the placed brands generated and whether the brand recall would translate into the purchase patterns of the Pakistani consumers.

3.2.1 Ontological positioning

Rageh, et al. (2013) states that the first step in designing a research is to evaluate the knowledge claims of the study, which refers to what and how the researcher would learn during the research, researchers make assertions about what is knowledge, which is known as ontology. The ontological positioning of this research is interpretive in nature as there are multiple realities and multiple meanings can be generated from the study which requires more than a single, structured mechanism, as the goal of social research is to study and develop an understanding of social life and discover how people construct meanings in their natural settings (Rageh, et al., 2013) thus the research has to be flexible in nature. Bell (cited in Asghar, 2012) points out that the interactions between indviduals results in social characteristics which are constantly changing and thus a flexible approach is required to assesand analyze these characteristics.

3.2.2 Epistemological positioning

How the researcher gains the knowledge is called the epistemology of research (Rageh, et al., 2013). The epsitemological positioning of this research is based on subjectivism as Bryman and Bell (cited in Asghar, 2012) point out that in the subjective approach what a researcher thinks important is the essence of this approach, which is further a characteristic of the qualitative approach to research.

3.2.3 Qualitative and Exploratory research positioning

As this research is about consumer perspectives and perceptions based on their associations with the James

Bond fandom, qualiatiave research design is more appropriate for this research as opposed to quantitative research which is not effective at understanding behavioural trends and perspectives as it chips away at heterogenity as quantitaive research methods are not sufficent to analyse intangibility (Asghar, 2012) as they are burdened by the constant urge to scrutinize emerging concepts for validity and generalizability, instead of judging in terms of speculative thought, imagination, representation (Kapoulas & Mitic, 2012) and hence the qualitative research methods are more suitable to unfold a phenomena (Rageh, et al., 2013) as qulitative methods provide a better insight or understanding to explore the phenomenon under investigation and help develop meanings by exploring experiences (Kapoulas & Mitic, 2012). Qualitative research does not provide a uniformity of numbers and equations as it uses words and images for its consious search of meanings *(ibid)*.

3.2.4 Inductive approach

Based on the nature of this research and its objective to explore how influential is the Bond brandscape in affecting the consumption patterns of its tribe members, an inductive research approach would be used, Neuman (cited in Rageh, et al., 2013) explains the inductive research where the researcher begins with detailed observations and moves towards more abstract generalizations and ideas which may highlight factors that were missing from the previous literature.

3.3 Data collection and techniques

In research the important aspect lies in what works as opposed to the methods or techniques that are used or applied to getting the answers, the problem is the most important part of any research, and the researchers are welcome to use all the approaches that would help in solving the problem (Creswell, 2003).

3.3.0 Triangulation approach

Over the years the researchers realizing that all methods and techniques have certain limitations decided to employ more than one research technique within a certain methodological design to get better solutions and reduce the bias that may hinder the research (Creswell, 2003). Kapoulas (cited in Kapoulas & Mitic, 2012) advocates ensuring credibility and trustworthiness when using qualitative research design, in his research he emphasizes the benefit of triangulation or multi methods to ensure checks and balances, his works are strongly supported by Miles and Huberman (cited in Kapoulas & Mitic, 2012) who highlight the importance of triangulation as the best means to getting the answers as seeing and hearing multiple sources and with the use of different methods the validity of the solutions can be ensured. Keeping that in mind this research incorporates a multi method qualitative approach and uses various techniques so as to get a better insight to the presented research problem. This research uses netnography to explore the impact of Bond movies across the online fandom, to understand the various aspects of Bond movies that the fandom members use to morph meanings in their daily lives. This research then incorporates the themes generated from the netnographic data to form an illlustrative case study that talks about and explains the various changes in terms of fashion and style Bond has undergone. Finally the researcher uses mood boards, a projective technique to understand how the Bond fashion is reflected in the tastes of Pakitani Bond fans.

3.3.1 Netnography

Caru and Cova (cited in Rageh, et al., 2013) explain that experience is a singular thing that happens to the consumers that can not be accessed by the researchers, and thus the researchers base their findings on the interpretations of their subjects, however qualitative techniques such as interviews and focus groups can have drawbacks such as respondent inhibition, qualitative techniques such as ethnography provide better insight into consumer experiences (Rageh, et al., 2013). Over the years the market oriented ethnographic methods have been used in an online context, Kozinets (2002) used the word 'netnography' as a qualitative method that adapts ethnographic techniques in an online context to study consumer behaviour and culture. It is argued that netnography is a very effective method to understand behaviour and experiences as the subjects are candid in their online narratives *(ibid)*. Kozinets (cited in Rageh, et al., 2013) explains the two important aspects of netnography are entrée and data collection, the first aspect involves finding online communities and fandoms that are most appropriate to the research, whereas the second aspect involves gathering the data from the online communities.

Elliott and Jankel-Elliot (cited in Rageh, et al., 2013) talk about netnography as a non participant observation based on online published consumer experiences, non participant observation reduces the chance of the opinions being influenced by the outsider. For the purpose of this study, the researcher intensively reviewed various fandoms and social media sites to gain an indepth insight into the views and opinions of all the Bond tribe members and their associations with different aspects of the film and its influences on the fandom members. The second aspect of netnographic techniques, the data collection was undertaken by recording and observing the online texts, images and opinions of the fandom members. As online contexts are a refrence to the adopted identity or self of the subject and not their real self thus using Kozinets (2002) guidelines the data collection was focused on the unit of analysis instead of focusing on the indviduals.

3.3.2 Case method

A case study research is based on an emperical inquiry that explores a contemprory phenomena in an indepth manner, and helps the researcher develop an insight into the research question or problem that the researcher

43

decides to explore (Farquhar, 2012). Case study research provides insights into what, who and how aspects of the research design and facilitate the researcher in getting better insights to unfold the phenomena of the chosen research problem *(ibid)*. For this research problem themes from the netnographic data were incorporated and the case method illustrates the fashion and accesory brands adopted in the Bond movies, the case study talks about the brands placed in the franchise and the fashion style and brands used solely based on the researcher's perspective inorder to consiously explore and enfold brand patronage in the film franchise. The researcher thus watched all the Bond movies in chronological order and a case study was developed based on the observations made, out of the six Bonds from the film franchise, the case study focuses on the three most popular and fashionably correct and relevant James Bond actors that were highlighted during the netnographic research namely: Sean Connery, Pierce Brosnan and Daniel Craig.

3.3.3 Mood boards (projective technique)

Staying true to the research objectives of exploring the various aspects of the Bond brandscape, and realizing that the data generated from netnographic techniques was a reflection of the subjects' adopted identities, so inorder to gauge whether the fashion brands in the Bond franchise generated enough recall and actually reflected the viewers consumption patterns, the projective technique were also used, which are techniques that involve the use of a stimuli that projects the participants deep seated or subjective beliefs using objects or people (Hofstede, et al., 2007). The projective techniques can be subdivided ino various techniques such as associations that connect the research objects with words, images or thoughts, the second aspect of projective techniques is completion of stories, sentences and arguments, the third subdivision is construction which includes answering questions about other people's behaviour, fourth aspect is choice ordering which ranks objects in terms of preferences and finally expression techniques that include creative techniques of role playing and drawing *(ibid)*.

The projective technique used in this study was the expression technique of mood boards, mood boards are collages containing multiple images that represent how consumers feel about the research problem (Hofstede, et al., 2007). In this study the researcher wanted to examine the consumer recall of the placed brands in the James Bond films, and whether the fashion brands influence the viewers enough to reflect their consumption patterns.

3.4 Data sampling and research techniques used

For the purpose of this research the sampling techniques and the research procedure adopted are explained as follows.

3.4.1 Sampling

For the projective techniques used in this research 8 Pakistani male respondents were selected using non probability sampling research methods, where the respondents are selected using non random methods, where human judgemnet affects the respondent selection as the chance of some respondents to be selected is greater than the others (Bryman & Bell, 2007).

The target population for the projective techniques used in this research constituted of Pakistani male respondents. Convenience sampling was used to choose the respondents who could easily be accessed and to get all the information promptly.

3.4.2 Research procedure

As this research was based on a multi method approach, netnography, case method and projective techniques were used for this research in order to gain insights into various aspects of the Bond brandscape. The first research technique used in this triangulation approach was netnography, the researcher wanted to explore the Brand associations people have with the Bond brandscape and whether the associations translated into the people's everyday lives or not. The researcher thus studied these associations in an online context by evaluating the virtual Bond tribes or fandoms. Various social networking websites such as twitter, pininterest, instagram and tumblr were used to search for the presence of Bond fandoms and the opinions of the fandom members in terms of words and pictures were used and evaluated inorder to gauge the strength of the Bond franschise in translating into the everyday lives of its fandom members and themes were generated that covered various pertinent aspects of the movies that the fandom members were affected by or talked about.

For the second approach in this traingulation research method, themes generated from the netnographic data were used to develop a case study that was based on observation and covered various aspects of the fashion trends in the movie. The researcher watched the twenty three Bond movies in the franchise and talked about the fashion statements made by three most popular actors of the the six who potrayed James Bond in the past fifty years, in terms of both the clothes and the accessories. The case study was the result of the researcher's observation and opinion based on the movies and browsing through the 007 website.

The researcher also wanted to study the Bond tribes success from a Pakistani persspective and as netnography generated results that reflected a global Bond brandscape thus a third research technique, mood boards which are a part of projective techniques were used, the researcher used an online domain for creating mood boards, moodshare.co, the researcher created a private domain for the purpose of this research jamesbondfashion.co, the male respondents were invited to join the domain as internal users who could access their indvidually assigned boards. Each board contained various images relating to men's wear and accessories, some of the images were the ones of brands patronized in the bond films. The male respondents were asked to name their favorite James Bond, choosing an actor from the three top actors found by the netnographic data analysis, pictures of whose clothes were there in the mood board's light box, the respondents were then asked to create a mood board or collage of images from the light box which reflected their personal style. Each saved collage incorporated the style sense of the respondent from the pictures presented in the light box.

3.5 Data Analysis

For the purpose of this research, coding was used where the collected data was assigned and arranged according to descriptive codes, in Qualitative research codes are basically words or phrases that assign a summative, salient attribute to the visual data that captures the essence of the collected data (Saldana, 2009). The assigned codes were then assigned to suitable categories and themes were generated from the categories. The codes, categories and the theming helped in organizing the data and helped the researcher in interpreting the data and making sense of the large ammount of the data that was collected. Emergent meanings from the data were then used to explore the themes in context of the nature of this research.

3.6 Ethical concerns

Though some researchers have argued about online information being a public domain and considered the use of online opinions without consent as acceptable (Rageh, et al., 2013) however certain ethical precautions were taken for this study based on Kozinets (2002) research guidelines, anonymity of all the fandom members was maintained throughout the study, caution was taken regarding the private vs public online texts, any direct quotations that were used in this study were with full consent of the respondents who were informed of the research and its implications, similarly when using the projective techniques consent forms were given to the respondents and their consent was sought, however the purpose of the research and its implications were not completely disclosed so as to get candid, unconsious opinions that would best reflect the respondents taste as opposed to consious answers that would be purposefully chosen to fit the research aims.

Chapter 4: What was discovered?

4. What was discovered

This chapter examines and analyzes the data that was collected in the course of this research; through all the triangulation techniques that were used.

4.1 Netnographic finings and data analysis

The netnographic data which was collected through various social networking sites in the form of both texts and images was assigned distinct descriptive codes. The codes dissected the James Bond brand into various elements and each element was studied and analyzed as an individual sub brand and how the fandom members felt about and related to the sub brands and morphed those elements to reflect their daily lives. Codifying and analysis of the coded data lead to noticing the patterns and linkages amongst the codes. The codes were then grouped into categories based on the similarities the codes shared. Upon analysis and comparison of the categories, certain themes were identified. The identified themes were based upon the perceptions and associations of the fandom members about the James Bond brandscape and its sub brands. The identified themes were as follows:

> The best Bond debate
> James Bond a fashion icon
> The aspired Bond lifestyle
> James Bond the original spy
> Bond locations as a tourist attraction
> Other James bond characters

The purpose was to use these themes to gauge the strength of the James Bond brand in creating a Bond tribe and how the various elements or themes played a role in developing and strengthening the tribe. The online James Bond tribe or fandom was analyzed based on the themes listed above to understand and analyze the opinions of the Bond fandom members to understand their feelings and associations with various aspects of James Bond brandscape and how the fandom members used various aspects or elements of James Bond to morph meanings and associations in their everyday lives. The themes listed above were used to study the data from various social networking sites and fandoms to understand the online James Bond tribes and the opinions of its members and the morphed meanings, self and social symbolism that the Bond movies created for its fandom members.

The best Bond debate

Codifying, categorizing and analysis of data from various social networking sites and fandoms lead to identification of a recurring debate as to which of the six actors from all twenty three movies was the most authentic James Bond. All the fandom members had differing views on the subject all of them having their own particular favourite with strong cases in the favour of and against their favourites and least favourite actors in the role. The fandom member's arguments were based on both actor and character traits and whether the actors were able to match up to the James Bond character of Ian Fleming's fantasy and if they their individuality and distinct personalities added to the character or fell short of the way the character was meant to be. The fandom members used words like: *the original bond, most authentic, most believable, and real; best looking and smooth* in their arguments for their favourite Bonds.

Sean Connery, the first actor to ever play James Bond was a favourite amongst most of the fandom members. He was one of the most tweeted about Bond actors and in many fandoms the members posted that Connery was their favourite. In an online Bond fandom one member posted that:

Although over the years each actor brought their own personalities and additional elements to the Bond character, but Connery had a blend of all elements that the other actors had, Connery had a certain flair that adds to the James Bond character and Connery was the original Bond and he had a unique face which will always be the face of James Bond.

On another fandom a Connery fan praising Connery talked about Connery's unique ability to portray James Bond saying that:

Connery's wry delivery was the most authentic and the most enjoyable, he nailed the debonair aspect but could transform into a deadly assassin in a moment

Daniel Craig had the second highest number of fans based on the netnographic data in the form of both images and texts. Many fandom members acknowledged Daniel Craig's Bond portrayal as the most authentic and closest to the character of Ian Fleming's fantasy. One fandom member highlighted this point by saying:

I believe Daniel Craig epitomizes the Bond that Fleming wrote about, a cold assassin who had his vulnerable moments

Whoever was cynical with Daniel Craig being cast as James Bond based on the first two movies changed their minds after the third as Skyfall helped eradicate all the reasons people have with disliking the last two movies. As Skyfall brought back all the elements that people associated with James Bond and expected to be there in all the movies of the franchise. As one fandom points out:

Skyfall sealed the deal for me proving why Craig was the best Bond and Skyfall the best movie of the franchise as it had all the elements that of the coarse new realism and old school James Bond.

James Bond in people's mind was an assassin and was supposed to depict that and act all terrifying as one fandom member points out:

Daniel Craig and Pierce Brosnan would be my top favourites, the Bond for me is someone who is a terrifying killer and these two delivered, Bond is a scary assassin with a massive body count and that isn't a man who is barrel of laughs

Most of the fandom member's point that their favourite Bond is someone they grew up with thus Brosnon was massively popular. He was considered smooth, stylish and a perfect assassin though not someone who was given the best movie scripts to work with and yet he delivered through his smoothness and the charisma he exuded. A fandom member said:

My number one would always be Connery, but to nominate a second I'd name the Bond I grew up with, sure he was in some bad scripted films, but he had the suave, he was the 'let me adjust my tie before I drive the tank through the city' Bond, and I love that

Based on the tweets and the fandom members' comments and polls, Pierce Brosnan was the third favourite followed by Roger Moore who was a close fourth, a Roger Moore fan talking about Moore's incredible style said:

Roger Moore's urbane tongue in cheek style made him the perfect Bond

The other two actors who played James Bond, Timothy Dalton and George Lezenby came at fifth and six according to the fandom polls and posts, Timothy Dalton was praised for his vulnerable side whereas Lezenby's one Bond movie was a favourite amongst the fandom members. The posts regarding those two Bonds were as follows:

As my ideal Bond I would pick Timothy Dalton's Bond from the Living Daylights. I like the fact that he's not a stone cold killer and has standards.

I really like George Lazenby his film is my favourite Bond movie.

James Bond a fashion icon

No matter which actor played the part, James Bond has been regarded as a style icon that most men look up to, especially when it comes to the tuxedo. Over the years the tuxedo has become synonymous with James Bond. On many social networking sites such as Twitter and instagram people used the James Bond reference with their photographs in a tuxedo or a suit. #jamesbond was a common thread on both Twitter and instagram with people's tuxedo photographs.

The impeccably dressed spy, has been a style template for men over the years, from Connery to Craig each Bond's suiting has been a style aspiration for many men. The James Bond Character and his many incarnations have been referred to as the best fashion muses in the history. The impact of the Bond tuxedo or suits has been too much to be calculated. *The Bond Suit* is a commonly used term across many social networking sites and fandoms. The members use the term *Bond suit* to talk about their fashion aspirations. One member talking about this said:

When I told my brother to get fitted for a tuxedo he said 'oh I should get a James Bond suit'

Another Bond fan posted:

The fiancée asked me what colour vest I would wear at the wedding, so she could match the flowers, and I was like what, James Bond doesn't wear a vest with his tuxedo, why would I

James Bond's style inspiration went beyond the tuxedo and the suit. The casual clothes he has worn over the years from Brosnon's jackets to Craig's sweater to his Levis jeans are iconic and much sought after. The Rolex and Omega watches that James Bond has worn over the years are a huge part of people's style inspiration. Across fandoms and many social networking sites people posted pictures of their proud purchases of the watches and shoes James Bond has worn over the years. At a fandom a member explained James Bond's role in being a style icon by saying:

James Bond has a great appeal as a style icon to hetro males because he is a perfect balance between an action dude and a chic gentleman, the clothes, the accessories, the gadgets it's all a part of the massive appeal

The aspired Bond lifestyle

Over the years James Bond has become a life style aspiration, an aspiration that goes beyond the way he dresses. The cars he drives, the gadgets he uses and the way he likes his drink all that is something that inspires the Bond fans. From the netnographic data many references to the Bond lifestyle were found. From the way James Bond introduced himself *Bond, James Bond* to the way he liked his vodka martinis *Shaken not stirred* the fandom members used these references with respect to tweets and instaposts about aspects from their daily lives. References to the Bond lifestyle using some of his one liner and catch phrases were there on many fandoms. People used their names the same way Bond used his for introductions, following the same *Bond, James Bond* style. Similarly *Shaken not stirred* was a commonly used term in the gathered netnographic data. Fans used this phrase constantly in reference to their drinks, whether it was alcohol or not. Twitter posts using this reference were:

Getting a James Bond martini, made right #shakennotstirred

Dad made hot chocolate that probably would give Judy from Santa Claus a run for her money #shakennotstirred

The cars James Bond drives are a huge part of his overall appeal. One cannot think of James Bond without thinking of the fast cars Bond drives whether it was the Lotus submarine, the Aston Martin DB5 or the Mercedes used in the movies. The netnographic data collected from the fandoms and social networking sites in the form of both texts and images had many references to the Bond cars. The references of the Bond cars varied from aspirations to appreciations. The tweets about cars from Bond movies included tweets about the newly auctioned Lotus submarine and all the excitement about it. The tweets also included cars that people appreciated and aspired to have including the BMW Z8 from the world is not enough and of course the classic Aston Martin DB5. One such tweet was:

Wow shocked to find that even a girly girl like me can appreciate the beauty of Aston Martin DB5

Another tweet about Aston Martin was:

Seeing the Aston Martin DB5 on the road made my day, Santa I want one please

James Bond the original spy

James Bond at the basic level was a spy, who risked his life for queen and country. Many fandom members saw him as that giving him a super hero status. The fandom members used the James Bond reference with actions of daring and adventure of their daily lives. Whether it was something they experienced or witnessed. Anything that had a super hero or adventurous vibe to it people used the James Bond reference to associate with it. Whether it was something adventurous and daring or super secret spy like. One tweet relating to the adventurous aspect of James Bond was:

The royal visitor will be arriving via a helicopter that is so James Bond

Another tweet was:

The best thing about Japan is I can imagine it having many James Bond like qualities

Similarly another tweet regarding secrecy and typical spy behaviour was:

All equipment and audio devices were sealed today totally James Bond style

Bond locations as a tourist attraction

Even though James Bond is quintessentially British and is presented as a British spy and that is a huge part of who James Bond is. People see James Bond as a British spy but James Bond is a globe trotter and travels to various locations for MI6's missions. From Jamaica to

Swiss Alps James Bond has travelled the world for his missions, the locations that James Bond travelled to have become a holiday aspiration for many people. The Bond fans have been to various Bond based locations from Brit movie tours in London to the Khao Pan King or James Bond Island from Roger Moore's man with the golden gun, to Contra dam in Swiss Alps, Meteora Agia Triada monastery in Greece from Moore's for your eyes only. From Thunderball Grotto in the Bahamas to Prague Czech Republic in Casino Royale, to the ninja training school in Japan from you only live twice. James Bond fans and fandom members have either visited or talked about visiting all the places from their favourite Bond movies. One fan posted a picture while sitting at Fontonbleu Miami Beach, and captioned the picture: *at the place where Bond and Goldfinger played cards*

Another fan tweeted:

Hong Kong here I come, visiting another Bond location

Other James bond characters

Not only James Bond but the other characters in the movies have become iconic and brands in their own right whether it is M, Q, Bond girls or the villains. Each character has become massively famous with the Bond fans and is discussed on fandoms and social networking sites. James Bond franchise has some of the most iconic villains whether it was Ernst Stavro Blofeld and his white pet cat, Emilio Largo and his eye patch, or oddjob and his hat. The Bond villains are iconic characters and brands in their own right and are frequently tweeted and posted about. One tweet about a bond villain was:

A man with an eye patch and an English accent is in the lobby of my building #bondvillain I think so

Another fan posted:

I keep picturing Saif in my head circling Tripoli in his convoy while rubbing his hands and crackling hysterically

Similarly the bond girls are also iconic and often posted about on both fandoms and social networking sites. The Bond girls are also an aspiration for the fandom members, the posts about Bond girls ranged from discussing the different Bond girls over the years, discussing their acting, the job description, their wardrobe and styling as well speculations about who the new Bond girl would be. The posts also included how people would love it if it was a real life job and would love to do it in real life. One such post was:

I would love to be a girl for one reason, be a bond girl

M the head of MI6 is also an icon and a brand in itself. M enjoys a massive level of popularity and M's quotes and sayings are often posted and tweeted. Speculations as to who would play the new M are also constantly trending on the different social networking sites and fandoms. One fan tweeted about M and Skyfall saying:

Seen Skyfall, did you know M's character was based upon Stella Remington the author of the Geneva trap

Q or the Quartermaster from the James Bond is also a much talked about character, the head of the Q branch division, who provides James Bond with weapons and high tech gadgets is also an icon in his own right. A fan post about Q was:

Feeling like Q from James Bond, I give the missions, the equipment and then I fade in the background

4.2 The case method

The first two themes from the netnographic findings: the best Bond debate and James Bond as a fashion icon were used and incorporated to form a case study. The case study used the top three most famous Bond actors Sean Connery, Pierce Brosnon and Daniel Craig and their fashion trends and preferences in the twenty three movies of the EON franchise. The following case study talks about fashion and style of James Bond. It sheds light on the changes in fashion trends in men's wear in the past fifty years and how James Bond has embraced the changing trends, the case also talks about the various accessories Bond adopted in the movies and discusses some of the product placements from the movies.

In James Bond's Closet

"Before Superman, Batman or Indiana Jones, there was Bond, the bespoke superhero, blowing up stuff and nonchalantly risking life and limb for God and country."
Hal Hinson

At the movies

Movies have a tendency of taking the viewers on a journey where the realities of their daily lives take a back seat and for two hours or so the viewer becomes totally engrossed in the larger than life stories being portrayed on the screens. The viewer forgets his or her problems and the mundane aspects of the daily life and puts himself/herself in the shoes of the onscreen characters and creates or interprets meanings from the movies. This journey at the movies is both emotional and aspiring. On one hand the viewer is on a roller coaster of emotions, where the viewer emotions keep constantly changing with the emotions of the on screen protagonist, and yet the movies invoke more than just emotional feelings, the viewer looks at the larger than life protagonist and takes aspirations from the larger than life characters, from the way the protagonist talks, carries himself, the clothes he wears and the brands he uses but what makes a character and the placed brands the character endorses memorable enough for the viewers to want to imitate it, does this wanting to imitate last after the movie ends and actually translates into purchase decisions of the viewers or the viewer's brand recall lasts only till the next movie and the next protagonist to be inspired from ?

In James bond's shoes

No matter how short term the viewer memory is, one protagonist that the viewers are not likely to forget about was born in Ian Fleming's fantasy and came to life on the movie screens in 1962, the impeccably dressed English spy James Bond, who wore a suit with the casual elegance that most men wear T-shirts, preferred his vodka martinis shaken and not stirred has lived for fifty plus years on cinema screens and made a lasting impression on the viewers whether it is in terms of his fashion statements, accessorizing or his preferences for cars. James Bond has been a fashion icon and aspirations for over fifty years, incorporating and embracing the changing fashions throughout the times and distinct style of each of the six men that portrayed James Bond over the years. The suits he has worn have become a template for men to design their suits based upon, the accessories he wears and the brands he patronizes have become an aspiration for the sort of lifestyle people want.

"Bond mistrusted anyone who tied his tie with a Winsor knot. It showed too much vanity, it was often the mark of a cad" Ian Fleming

The 60's.....In Connery's Derby Suede

The first time we are introduced to James Bond, in Dr No. even before the Scottish actor Sean Connery utters the famous words *Bond.... James Bond* and before we see Sean Connery's face; our first glimpse of James Bond is of the silk turn back cuff of his evening suit, which has been regarded as a signature style Ian Fleming chose for his own suits. Sean Connery's James Bond was authentically British in fashion, style as well as attitude. Anthony Sinclair was responsible for James Bond's conduit cut suits. Even though this isn't mentioned in the movie however in Dr No, Sean Connery throws in a reference of Savile Row when asked of his tailor; Bond replies *I have a man in Savile Row.* When Sean Connery was chosen as James Bond he wasn't used to wearing suits, Ian Fleming's own tailor who designed Connery's suits and the director of the movie had Connery wear suits all the time before production started, he even slept in suits to master the disdain that is natural to the British when it comes to fine clothing. Conduit suits are very British with a two buttoned, single breasted jacket, with natural shoulders, full chest and slender waist and slightly flared skirt, forward English pleats in the pants, the suits were lightweight and conservative in colour as a spy is supposed to fit in the crowd not stand out. The suits Bond wears are mostly grey, charcoal or navy blue; when Bond wears blue he wears all blue, except for the white handkerchief and black shoes without laces. The first time we see Connery's monochrome navy on navy look is when he is sitting in M's office. Besides the suits and the formal attire, Sean Connery was seen in slacks and polo shirts when he was on assignments and where suits would've seemed inappropriate and he carried those off with as much grace as he carried off suits. Sean Connery's Bond is very English and reflects the inverted snobbery that the English are known for. No matter how wealthy the British are they shudder at the displays of this wealth, thus Bond's impeccable suits display comfort, his Rolex looks worn and used, his Bentley has an ageing look to it, even when Q gives Bond an Aston Martin DB5 in *Goldfinger* the car is grey unlike the shiny yellow Phantom of Goldfinger. Which is a recurring theme in the earlier Bond movies, James Bond though is an ex navy man who is provided expensive clothes and gadgets by the Government for his services yet Bond is a refined English gentleman who knows his wine and knows car brands and clothe labels yet he doesn't display those labels unlike the villains in the movies because that would be too vulgar for an English gentleman. Red Grant may display the brand of his gold watch, Count Lippe may drive a shiny purple Bentley and brag about his suits but James Bond is too English to bother with displaying labels and choosing loud vulgar colours.

Bond in the 70's and 80's

From 60's to 90's James Bond went through various changes, three actors portrayed James Bond after Connery, George Lezenby, Roger Moore and Timothy Dalton. Each Bond added his own signature to the Bond look and the designers incorporated the current fashion trends in the look. In the 70's, fashion was all about extremes, loud colours, sequences, tight fitted trousers with elephant legs even for men and expression of self through clothes was all clothes had to incorporate. James bond in the 70's remained authentic though, the gala outfit remained the same but current trends were subtly incorporated in the look by adding ruffles to the shirts, and the other suits were changed in the cut, with wider trousers. Turtle necks and safari suits that became a signature look for Moore were added to the wardrobe, along with six button jackets with formal suits. In the 80's fashion gain a newfound importance, labels became important along with bolder, brighter colours. The fashion changes were incorporated in the Bond movies adding large shouldered power suits. The three piece suits went out of fashion, the high six buttons on jackets went out of style replaced by low four button jackets, the lapels became narrower, pinstripes returned to fashion, trousers became loose fit neckties became narrower, skinny ties often leather skinny ties became trendy.

The 90's…..In Brosnan's Church's Presley

In the 90's fashion took a whole new phase, fashion became all about self expression; tattoos, body piercing and t-shirts with slogans became the norm. The 80's power suits were replaced by sleek three and sometimes four button suits, leather jackets cut in the style of formal coats became fashionable. At this time Pierce Brosnan was cast as James Bond; the traditional English suits were abandoned in the favour of well cut, sleek Brioni Italian suits, with three button jackets, wide lapels, reverse pleated pants, larger and louder butterfly black bow ties and pinstripes. Unlike his contemporaries Pierce Brosnan's Bond didn't shy away from colours and was seen in loud colour ties. Brosnan was the most formally dressed Bond, casual clothing meant less formal and not exactly casual, with linen suits and cravats, the suits were paired with knee length overcoats that seemed more appropriate for the English weather, a leather jacket was also added to the Bond wardrobe and Bond's beloved Rolex was switched to Omega and an occasional dalliance from Aston Martin towards BMW was there in the Brosnan era. Pierce Brosnan undoubtedly became the best dressed on screen man there ever was, but unlike his contemporaries Brosnan always stood out of the crowd instead of fitting in with the surroundings unlike Connery, Lazenby, Moore or Dalton. Pierce Brosnan was too elegant for a spy and looked more like a business tycoon.

The 2000's......In Craig's Crocket & Jones Tetbury

The film makers made some bold moves with Bond fashion in the post Brosnan era, with Daniel Craig the first blonde and blue eyed Bond, who was brooding, wounded and questioned himself. For his first movie Casiono Royale the film makers broke away from the suit becoming the essence of Bond, and Craig's Bond brought an element of authenticity and was a closer reflection to the James Bond that Fleming wrote than any other Bond had ever been, except perhaps Connery. Sean Connery's Bond wore impeccably tailored suits however he knew when to dress in casuals and he had the ability to blend in the crowd and same was the case with Craig. Craig's

Bond is not afraid to discard the suit in the action scenes unlike his predecessors, he wears a suit when it is required and appropriate when the script legitimately demands it, and carries it off well, whether it is the Brioni suits in *Casino Royale* or Tom Ford suits in *Qunatum of Solace* and *Skyfall*. Tom Ford suits are the most impressive suits compared to all the preceding designers, the suits perfectly incorporate Italian class and American minimalism. The material and the detailing give a class to the simplistic design. Shorter jackets, with a perfect fit, with two buttons worn lower than usual; the lapels are replaced by a shawl. The suit trousers are low cut and have a flat front. The Craig era saw a lot of changes to the classic Bond as we knew him, the aristocratic British air that James Bond always had was somewhat Americanized, the product placements used were not the premium Brand placements of before. The James Bond who preferred shaken Vodka Martinis and an occasional Dom Perignon was seen sipping Heineken beer, Sony became an official sponsor and all the gadgets used in the movies were by Sony. In Skyfall the phone Bond uses to talk to M was Sony Xperia TL.

Tipping the hat to James Bond

In the fifty years of his presence, James Bond has become a style icon, in terms of both the clothes he wears, whether they are the formal wear or casual clothing and the brands he endorses. Skyfall the 23rd movie in the EON franchise was a tribute to the fifty years of James Bond and had the most promotional tie-ins. The in-film nods to the previous movies were evident in many aspects of the movie the tombstones of Bond's were from *You Only Live Twice*. Bond's Scottish heritage comes from Fleming's later novels, which was Fleming's tribute to Connery. Travelling through the Scottish altitudes is a nod to the chase scene from *Goldfinger* where Bond's Aston Martin chases Goldfinger's Rolls Royce through the Swiss Alps. All the in-film nods are a subtle and yet nostalgic reminder of the essence of James Bond, the iconic English spy.

4.3 Analysis of the mood boards

Mood boards created by the eight chosen respondents and generated through moodshare.co were analyzed to see whether the respondent's favourite James Bond actor impacted their sense of style or not. As explained in the previous chapter each respondent was asked to name a favourite James Bond actor, choosing an actor from the three used for this research namely Sean Connery, Pierce Brosnan and Daniel Craig. These three actors were chosen for this research because based on the netnographic data gathered of the fandom these three were the most popular actors to portray James Bond. The generated mood boards were compared with a fashion timeline (see appendix 2) that portrayed various fashion styles adopted by James Bond over the years, the clothes and accessories from the timeline representing fashion styles of the three actors were there in the domain's lightbox for the respondents to choose from along with other clothes and accessory options from other well known brands not used in the Bond franchise. Of the eight chosen respondents' one respondent named Sean Connery as his favourite, whereas two named Pierce Brosnan as their favourite and five chose Daniel Craig. The generated mood boards were then analyzed to see patterns and see if the respondents would pick clothes and accessories worn by their favourite actors or not.

Sean Connery

One respondent, respondent A, named Sean Connery as his favourite James Bond actor. The light box contained various clothes and accessory options that were worn by Sean Connery in the movies. The respondent's mood board was analyzed to see whether his fashion preferences reflected the fashion style of Sean Connery. The respondent's choice of clothes incorporated the clothes that Sean Connery wore in his movies (see Appendix 3). The respondent chose a three piece conduit cut English suit that Connery had worn in the movies, along with the Slazenger sweater and a terry cloth Polo shirt both of which Connery had worn. However the shoes and accessories that the respondent chose for his mood board were not the ones worn by Connery, the shoes that the respondent picked were Brosnan's Church's Presleys, the watch and tie the respondent A chose were both worn by Craig and were of Omega and Tom Ford respectively. The Sun glasses chosen by the respondent were Raybans not used in any of the Bond movies.

Pierce Brosnan

Of the eight respondents two respondents B and C said that Pierce Brosnon was their favourite James Bond. Their mood boards were again analyzed to gauge the style impact of Brosnon on their fashion preferences. The mood board created by the respondent B (see Appendix 4) had no resemblances to any fashion styles adopted by Pierce Brosnan. The respondent B chose an Armani tuxedo not used in any of the Bond movies and a Tom Ford suit that was worn by Daniel Craig. Respondent B also chose Crocket & Jones shoes that were worn by Daniel Craig. The respondent also picked a Hugo boss tie, an Armani watch, a Versace sun glasses none of which were used in any of the Bond movies.

The third respondent, respondent C's mood board incorporated many of the fashion choices adopted by Pierce Brosnan (see Appendix 5). The respondent picked Brioni's Italian cut tuxedo that was worn by Pierce Brosnan, along with Brosnan's Church's Presley shoes and Turnbull and Asser shirt that was worn by both Connery and Brosnon. However the tie that the respondent chose was Craig's Tom Ford and the chosen watch was Craig's Omega Planet Ocean 600M. The sun glasses that the respondent chose were Gucci not used in any of the Bond movies.

Daniel Craig

Daniel Craig was the most famous Bond actor amongst the respondents as five of the chosen eight respondents chose him as their favourite Bond actor. Respondent D's mood board was analyzed to see patterns and whether the patterns reflected Craig's fashion styles or not. Respondent D's mood board incorporated various elements of Craig's fashion statements from the Bond movies (see Appendix 6). The respondent picked Craig's Tuxedo from Tom Ford, along with Craig's tie and sun glasses both of which were Tom Ford designs. The shoes that the respondent picked were again Craig's Crocket & Jones. Besides the fashion and accessories brands patronized by Daniel Craig, respondent D also picked a Turnbull and Asser grenadine tie that was a Connery classic and a leather jacket by Angels and Berman that Brosnon wore. Respondent D's fashion choices also included Gucci sunglasses, Armani and a Diesel watch, and Ralph Lauren jeans and a CK shirt none of which were used in the Bond movies.

Respondent E's mood board only resemblance to Daniel Craig's fashion styling was the Crocket & Jones shoes (see Appendix 7). The tuxedo respondent E chose was Brosnon's Brioni tuxedo, the respondent also picked two suits Connery's English conduit suit and another Prada suit not from either of the actor's style. Respondent E chose two watches, Connery's Rolex Submarine and an Armani watch. Respondent E chose two more shoes, Brosnon's Chruch's Presley and Alferd Sergeant Shoes not from the movies. The sunglasses that respondent chose were Connery's wayfarers and another Gucci glasses not from the movies, the tie that the respondent chose was Connery's classic Turnbull and Asser grenadine. The respondent also chose Ralph Lauren cashmere and a Fendi sweater, and an Armani shirt not from the movies.

Respondent F's fashion choices (see Appendix 8) included Daniel Craig's white Diesel jeans and Crocket & Jones shoes. The tuxedo the Respondent chose was the Brioni worn by Brosnon. The respondent also picked Connery's Derby Suede shoes, his Wayfarer sunglasses, and the Rolex Submarine watch. The respondent also chose other sunglasses Raybans and an Armani shirt not from the movies.

The respondent G chose two tuxedos' (see Appendix 9) one was Tom Ford worn by Craig, and the other one was

Brioni that Brosnon wore. The respondent also chose a Conduit suit that Connery had worn and also a Prada suit that was not used in the movies. Respondent F chose two Tom Ford ties worn by Craig, Tunrbull and Asser grenadine worn by Connery and another Hermes tie not from the movies. The watches respondent F chose did not include Craig's watch but included Connery's Rolex Submarine, Brosnon's Omega 300 M and a Diesel watch not from the movies. The respondent picked Craig's Crocket Jones shoes but also Connery's Derby Suede and Vass shoes not from the movies. The sunglasses that the respondent chose did not include Craig's sunglasses, the sunglasses that the respondent chose were Connery's wayfarers, Raybans, Gucci sunglasses. The respondent chose Tom Ford Shawl Cardigan worn by Craig and also Pierce Brosnan's Angel and Berman leather jacket. Respondent F chose Zara Youth shirt worn by Craig and CK, Gucci and Diesel shirts and Ralph Lauren jeans not from the movies.

Respondent H's fashion inspirations from Daniel Craig (see Appendix 10) reflected in his choices of the Tom Ford tuxedo, the Tom Ford tie and Crocket & Jones shoes. The respondent also picked Connery's Derby Suede shoes, a CK watch and Gucci sunglasses not from the movies.

Chapter: 5 At the end.....

5. At the end

This final Chapter takes into account the findings from the previous chapters and sums up the conclusions drawn from the multi methods used in this study. This chapter compares the findings from the online fandom and the empirical testing of impact of James Bond's fashion and brand patronage to the Pakistani Bond fans. In order to understand the similarities and differences that is there in the global fandom and the Pakistani Bond tribe. The netnographic findings indicated the interest and morphed meanings different aspects of the Bond franchise had for its fans, whereas projective techniques were used to explore whether the fashion and styles of James Bond translated into purchase aspirations of Pakistani consumers.

5.1 Summing up the Netnographic findings

The netnographic findings indicated that there is a strong James Bond fandom or tribe. The James Bond franchise is a very strong brand and not only that many aspects of the movies are brands in their own right. Whether it is James Bond as a character or other characters that are a part of the franchise, be it M, Q, Bond girls or the villains all of the characters have a massive appeal and influence on the fandom members. The fandom members draw aspiration from all the characters from the movie franchise and many brands have used that aspect to draw people towards their products. Like swatch watches came up with a collection of watches that was aspired by the Bond villains over the years. Each watch was designed reflecting the personality or the persona of the different Bond villains over the years and the concept was a huge success amongst the Bond fans.

The likeability of all the characters from the Bond franchise, no character has the same influence on the audience and the fans as the protagonist himself; James Bond's character over the years has had a huge appeal for the audience over the years. The impeccably dressed spy with his smooth manners and wry sense of humour has not only won the hearts of many by fighting the bad guys but has also set a standard for what men aspire to be. James Bond at the core level is a spy who fights antagonists for queen and country and people or fans associate that with him. Fans use the James Bond reference when talking about anything super secret or action based from the events of their daily lives no matter how small or big the thing is. James Bond's character has that action hero or super hero vibe to it and the reference of that is constantly used by the fans no matter who their favourite actor to portray Bond is the character references are there and much talked about.

Of all the six actors who portrayed James Bond over the years, the fandom members had their personal favourites and this was a much debated about topic across the fandom. Connery was the favourite with most fandom members, he was the first Bond and thus people easily associated his face with the title, his portrayal of Bond was thoroughly English, classic and much liked by the people who claimed that all the other actors were second spot contenders and could not touch Connery no matter what. Daniel Craig was easily the second favourite, he had a high recall being the current Bond and was much appreciated as many fans said that Craig's Bond came closest to depicting the spy Fleming wrote about he was a tough spy but had his vulnerable moments. Brosnan was also a huge fan favourite, his smooth manner and the way he carried his suit was really liked by the fans. Whereas Moore's eyebrow lift and manner was something that people enjoyed and talked about as a part of his appeal.

James Bond's larger than life character has a massive appeal the fans not only talk about the cars he drives and the locations he travels to fight off bad guys but they aspire to visit those places and drive those cars. The Bond cars are a much talked about or posted about phenomena Top Gear's show about all the cars used in the Bond franchise had really high ratings and was much appreciated and tweeted about. In the same way when Bond's Submarine Lotus was auctioned, the thread trended for days and there was a lot of excitement and speculations based on the possible bidder and how people wished to get that car. Of all the cars Bond drove over the years, the Aston Martin DB5 the classic Bond car is the fan favourite and is much tweeted and posted about. The tweets and posts range from appreciation of the car and flaunting the merchandize inspired by that car, in the form of key chains or souvenirs.

James Bond at a basic level is regarded as a super hero who fights bad guys in the same way that superman or spider man do, but unlike those super heroes James Bond's costume is an impeccably tailored suit. The suits that James Bond has worn over the years have become a style template for the men to design their suits or tuxedos based upon. Men see James Bond in his impeccably tailored suits and they want to wear what he wears even if they can't get the high tech gadgets as accessories to fight men who chase after world domination. The appeal of the suits James Bond wore was seen across the fandom, the fans not only talked about how beautifully tailored the Bond suits were but also how they got their suits made by the same designers and how the Bond suit was a template to base their suit designs upon. The Winsor knot in ties and vests with tuxedo was a thought that the fans shuddered at because the aversion that James Bond has of Winsor knots and how he never wore a vest with his tuxedo.

All the brands that Bond has adopted over the years be it Anthony Sinclair, Brioni, Tom Ford when it came to suiting, Turnbull and Asser shirts or Rolex and Omega watches were much talked about, had a high recall and likeability. Some of the Brand offerings that James Bond has worn over the years were iconic and had a huge appeal to them, be it the classic Anthony Sinclair conduit cut suit that Sean Connery wore, his Slazenger sweater, the grenadine tie or the pale blue Polo shirt. In the same way Brosnon's Brioni's Tuxedo, his Angels and Berman leather jacket were iconic and much talked about. In the same way the fans talked about Craig's classic Tom Ford Tuxedo, his Tom Ford shawl cardigan and the white Levis jeans he wore.

5.2 Summing up the findings from mood boards

The majority of the Pakistani respondents used for this research named Daniel Craig as their favourite actor out of the six actors who played James Bond for the EON franchise. Five out of the eight respondents named Daniel Craig as their favourite, two named Pierce Brosnon and one named Sean Connery. The mood boards that the respondents made were then analyzed to see whether they reflected the styles of the respondent's favourite Bond actors as explained in the previous chapter.

Upon reflections of the findings from the previous chapter, mixed results were noted. Majority of the respondents chose the tuxedos or suits worn by their favourite actors, however some respondents who named Craig as their favourite actor picked the Brioni tuxedo worn by Brosnon. The Brioni tuxedo was the tuxedo most of the respondents chose irrespective of the James actor they named as their favourite.

The results when it came to accessories such as ties, watches, sunglasses and shoes were not as influenced by the respondent's favourite actors as the tuxedos and the suits. majority of the respondents chose Tom Ford ties, crocket and Jones, Church's Presley shoes and Omega watches regardless of whether their favourite Bonds wore them or not and in most cases the respondents who named Brosnon and Connery as their favourites chose Craig's shoes and vice versa. The sunglasses that the respondents chose however were mostly not from the brands that the Bond actors had worn.

When it came to the casual clothes some of the respondents totally ignored that category and the one who chose casual clothes only a few chose the ones from their favourite Bond actors. One respondent chose Craig's Levis jeans, one respondent chose Craig's Zara shirt and one respondent chose Connery's blue polo these were the only casual clothes from the respondent's favourite actors. The rest of the mood board's casual clothing options were either from the different actor than the one the respondents named but in most cases people chose different brands than the ones from the movies.

5.3 Comparison of the Bond fandom and the Pakistani respondents

The netnographic study of the online fandom and social networking sites indicted a presence of a very strong global Bond tribe. The fans were impressed by and aspired from various aspects of the James Bond franchise. The fans not only talked about the various aspects of the movies but also aspired to adopt the James Bond lifestyle and that was reflected in the Brands they patronized and used whether it was the technological brands, cars, drinks or fashion brands. James Bond has had a huge impact on men's fashion wear and the fans regarded the clothes he wore and the accessories he used in a very good light. The suit and tuxedos were a huge part of James Bonds fashion style however the accessories especially the watches and even the casual clothes were given equal importance and enjoyed almost the same recall as the suiting and the designers responsible for the suiting. The Rolex and Omega watches and the cardigans, the shirts and jackets each Bond actor has worn over the years have become iconic brands that are much sought after.

The empirical study of the Pakistani respondents indicated that the James Bond tribe's presence was very strong in Pakistan and the respondents were influenced by James Bond's fashion sense however the fashion aspirations from James Bond were mostly with respect to the suiting and tuxedos and the accessories the different actors have patronized and adopted over the years were not reflected in the respondents fashion choices.

5.4 Implications of this research

Brand placement is a much talked about concept in the modern field of marketing however very few researches have actually sought to test the impact these Brand placements have on the consumers or fans. This study explored the success of Brand placement with respect to the James Bond franchise. The research used the fashion and styling aspect of James Bond to understand how the respondent used the fashion and style statements of James Bond to morph meanings of self identity in their daily lives. The sample size of this research however was very small and the same study can be used on a larger number of respondents to effectively understand the concept in a broader perspective. The research also just used James Bond's fashion and style to study its impact on men's wear, the research can be broadened to cover the fashion aspects and style of Bond girls to study female fashion based on the accessories patronized by other characters such as Bond girls. The research can also be broadened to include brand placements of other placed brands in the movies such as technological brands, cars, drinks and so on. Similar studies can be conducted using other movies to study brand placements and its impact on the respondents and their purchase patterns.

Bibliography

1. Asghar, K., 2012. *Branding Pakistan, A Pakistani student's perspective*. s.l.:LAP Lambert Academic Publishing .

2. Bloemer, J., Brijs, K. & Kasper, H., 2009. The CoO-ELM model A theoretical framework for the cognitive processes underlying country of origin-effects. *European Journal of Marketing*, 43(1/2), pp. 62-89.

3. Bryman, A. & Bell, E., 2007. *Business Research Methods*. second ed. s.l.:Oxford University Press.

4. Chryssochoidis, G., Krystallis, A. & Perreas, P., 2007. Ethnocentric beliefs and country-of-origin (COO) effect Impact of country, product and product attributes on Greek consumers' evaluation of food products. *European Journal of Marketing*, 41(11/12), pp. 1518-1544.

5. Cova, B., Pace, S. & Park, D. J., 2007. Global brand communities across borders: the Warhammer case. *International Marketing Review*, 24(3), pp. 313-329.

6. Creswell, J. W., 2003. *RESEARCH DESIGN Qualitative, Quantitative. and Mixed Methods Approaches*. London : SAGE Publications International Educational and Professional Publisher.

7. Delassus, V. P. & Descotes, R. M., 2012. Brand name substitution and brand equity transfer. *Journal of Product & Brand Management*, 21(2), p. 117–125.

8. Dionı́sio, P., Leal, C. & Moutinho, L., 2008. Fandom affiliation and tribal behaviour: a sports marketing application. *Qualitative Market Research: An International Journal,* 11(1), pp. 17-39.

9. Dowd, J. J., 2003. Films and Utopia the culture industry revisited. In: *Critical theory: diverse objects, diverse subjects.* s.l.:Elseiver Sceience Ltd, pp. 99-129.

10. Farquhar, J. D., 2012. *Case Study Research for Business.* s.l.:Sage Publication.

11. Felix, R., 2012. Brand communities for mainstream brands: the example of the Yamaha R1 brand community. *Journal of Consumer Marketing,* 29(3), p. 225–232.

12. Hofstede, A., Hoof, J. v., Walenberg, N. & Jong, M. d., 2007. Projective techniques for brand image research Two personification-based methods explored. *Qualitative Market Research: An International Journal,* 10(3), pp. 1352-2752.

13. Hudson, S. & Tung, V. W. S., 2010. "Lights, camera, action...!" Marketing film locations to Hollywood. 28(2), pp. 188-205.

14. Kapoulas, A. & Mitic, M., 2012. Understanding challenges of qualitative research: rhetorical issues and reality traps. *Qualitative Market Research: An International Journal,* 15(4), pp. 354-368.

15. Ko, E. & Lee, S., 2013. CINDERELLA STORYTELLING IN 21ST CENTURY: INTERPRETING POPULAR CULTURE IN THE MOVIES VIA VISUAL

NARRATIVE ARTS. *Advances in Culture, Tourism and Hospitality Research,,* Volume 7, pp. 91-99.

16. Kozinets, R. V., 2002. The field behind the screen: using netnography for marketing research in online communities. *Journal of Marketing Research,* Volume 39, pp. 61-72.

17. Lazarevic, V., 2012. Encouraging brand loyalty in fickle generation Y consumers. *YOUNG CONSUMERS,* 13(1), pp. 45-61.

18. Lee, T. D., Sung, Y. & Gregorio, F. d., 2010. Cross-cultural challenges Cross-cultural challenges. *Marketing Intelligence & Planning,* 29(4), pp. 366-384.

19. Ligorio, T., 2004. SHORT PAPER Postmodernism and fuzzy systems. *Kybernetes,* 33(8), pp. 1312-1319.

20. Lord, K. R. & Gupta, P. B., 2010. Response of buying-center participants to B2B product placements. *Journal of Business & Industrial Marketing,* 25(3), pp. 188-195.

21. Lysikova, O., 2012. FASHIONS IN TOURISM: THE VIEWS OF RUSSIAN TOURISTS AND EXPERTS. *Advances in Culture, Tourism and Hospitality Research,* Volume 6, pp. 195-204.

22. Mitchell, C. & Imrie, B. C., 2011. Consumer tribes: membership, consumption and building loyalty. *Asia Pacific Journal of Marketing and Logistics,* 23(1), pp. 39-56.

23. Moor, L., 2007. *The Rise of Brands.* UK : Berg.

24. Muzellec, L., Lynn, T. & Lambkin, M., 2012. Branding in fictional and virtual environments. 46(6), pp. 811-826.

25. Nittins, T., 2011. *Selling James Bond: Product Placement in the James Bond Films.* Newcastle: Cambridge Scholars Publishing.

26. O'Reilly, D. & Kerrigan, F., 2013. A View To A Brand: Introducing The Film Brandscape. *European Journal of Marketing* , 47(5/6).

27. Panayiotou, A., 2012. Deconstructing the manager: discourses of power and resistance in popular cinema. 31(1), pp. 10-26.

28. Pandey, S., 2012. Using popular movies in teaching cross-cultural management. *European Journal of Training and Development,* 36(2/3), pp. 329-350.

29. Perez, ,. M. E., Castan~o, R. & Quintanilla, C., 2010. Constructing identity through the consumption of counterfeit luxury goods. *lQualitative Market Research: An International Journa,* 13(3), pp. 219-235.

30. Rageh, A., Melewar, T. & Woodside, A., 2013. Using netnography research method to reveal the underlying dimensions of the customer/tourist experience. 16(2), pp. 126-149.

31. Saldana, J., 2009. *The Coding Manual for Qualitative Researchers.* London: Sage Publications.

32. Soller, Kurt (2011) style secrets to steal from 40 years of James Bond available at: http://www.esquire.com/the-

side/style-guides/james-bond-style-2011#slide-1 (accessed: 05.11.13)

33. Salzer, M. M. & Strannegård, L., 2010. Ain't misbehavin' – consumption in a moralized brandscape. *Marketing Theory,* 7(4), pp. 407-425.

34. Sementelli, A., 2009. Images in public administration: using popular media to bridge theories and practices. *Journal of Management Development,* 28(7), pp. 607-62.

35. Shankar, A., Elliott, R. & Fitchett, J. A., 2009. Identity, consumption and narratives of socialization. *Marketing Theory,* 9(75).

36. Simmons, G., 2008. Marketing to postmodern consumers: introducing the internet chameleon. *European Journal of Marketing,* 42(3/4), pp. 299-310.

37. Spector, B., 2008. The Man in the Gray Flannel Suit in the executive suite American corporate movies in the 1950s. *Journal of Management History,* 14(1), pp. 87-104.

38. Thurau, T. H., Houston, M. B. & Walsh, G., 2006. The Differing Roles of Success Drivers Across Sequential Channels: An Application to the Motion Picture Industry. 34(4), pp. 559-575.

39. Walsh, M. F., Winterich, K. P. & Mittal, V., 2010. Do logo redesigns help or hurt your brand?. *Journal of Product & Brand Management,* 19(2), p. 76–84.

40. Weiner, R. G., Whitfield, B. L. & Becker, J. T. "., 2011. *James Bond in World and Popular Culture.* Texas: Texas Tech Liabraries.

41. Wiley, N., 2003. EMOTION AND FILM THEORY. In: *Studies in Symbolic Interaction.* s.l.:Elsevier Science Ltd, p. 169–187.

42. Woodside, A. G., Sood, S. & Muniz, K. M., 2013. CREATING AND INTERPRETING VISUAL STORYTELLING ART IN EXTENDING THEMATIC APPERCEPTION TESTS AND JUNG'S METHOD OF INTERPRETING DREAMS. *Advances in Culture, Tourism and Hospitality Research,* Volume 7, p. 15–45.

Appendices

Appendix 1:

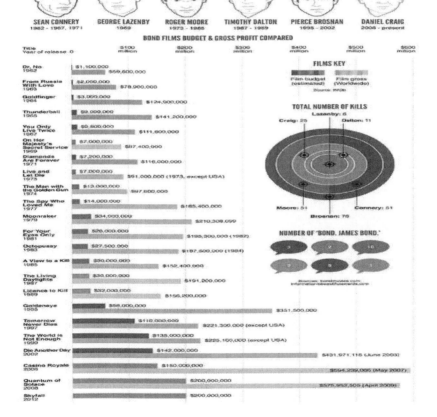

Appendix 2: James bond fashion timeline

Sean Connery 1960's

Tuxedo Anthony Sinclair

Formal: Anthony Sinclair

Casual: Orlebar Terry cloth polo

Sweater Slanzenger Burgundy V neck ribbed sleeves

Watch: Rolex Submarine 6538

Sunglasses Wayfarers

Pierce Brosnan 1990's

Formal: Brioni

Tuxedo: Brioni

Casual: Angels & Berman
leather jacket

Sunglasses: Persol PE2672-S

Sweater: Ballantyne cashmere

Watch: Omega seamaster

Daniel Craig 2000's

Tuxedo: Tom Ford

Formal: Tom Ford

Casual: Levis 306STA-PREST slacks

Sweater: Tom Ford shawl collar cardigan

Watch: omega seamaster Planet Ocean 600m

Sunglasses: Tom Ford Aviator TF108

Appendix: 3

Appendix: 4

Appendix: 5

Appendix: 6

Appendix: 7

Appendix: 8

Appendix: 9

Appendix: 10

Printed in Great Britain
by Amazon.co.uk, Ltd.,
Marston Gate.